place picture here

Presented to:

Leslie Larice Randalls

print name here

written by
Linda M. Washington

illustrated by
Julie Chen

a piece of MY mind™

It's Me, LESLIE

TYNDALE KiDS

Tyndale House Publishers, Inc.
Wheaton, Illinois

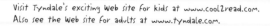

Visit Tyndale's exciting Web site for kids at www.cool2read.com.
Also see the Web site for adults at www.tyndale.com.

 Edited by Betty Free
Designed by Jackie Noe

A Piece of My Mind is a trademark of Tyndale House Publishers, Inc.

Also in the series A Piece of My Mind:
Just Plain Mel

ISBN: 0-8423-5373-9

Printed in Italy
12 11 10 09 08 07 06 05 04 03 02
10 9 8 7 6 5 4 3 2 1

FOR THE WOMEN IN MY FAMILY,

especially my mother—Susie L. Washington;

my grandmother—Marie Williams;

my sisters-in-law—Gia and Lisa; my nieces—Jasmine, Samantha, Megan, and Kathryn;

and other extended family members—Lillie and Samuel Huff; Vida Huff Donermeyer; Tamika Huff.

Also for my good friends Joyce Dinkins, Karen Massey, Kim Yow Harris,

Rita Lewis Perry, and Lisa Jackson;

and for my first best friend and writing partner, Donna Coleman

 LMW

May 28

Journal of Leslie Larice Randalls

Age: 11
Where I live: 472 Jefferson Place, Hillside Park, IL

LESLIE

This is Tuesday, and it's the **WORST** day of my life. Worse than the day I threw up at school because of the stomach flu. (And that was the day I found out my favorite TV show was canceled.)

Mama told me today that everything's ~~definite~~ definite (her favorite word). She and Daddy have been checking it out, and now

We're going to Eagle Rock Bible Church.

I was so mad when she told me. I hate change!

♪ ♪ ♪ ♪♪ ♪

**MAMA MADE ME MAD
SO I FEEL SAD
'CAUSE IT HURTS SO BAD**

I could write a whole **RAP** song about how TERRIBLY HORRIBLE everything is. I asked Mama why we had to change churches. I know it's just because they don't like the way the pastor runs the church. Ever since our old pastor died and his son (Rev. Samuels, Jr.) became pastor,

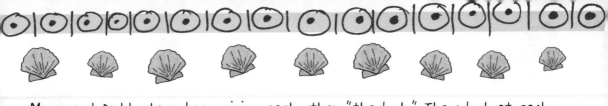

Mama and Daddy have been giving each other "the look." They look at each other a certain way when somebody says something they don't like.

Our pastor at New Salem has been the pastor for eight months now. Two months ago, I saw Mama and Daddy give each other "the look" five times in church.

That was a new record. I knew they were upset about something the pastor said. So the Sunday after that, we visited Eagle Rock Bible Church. That's the church Grampa goes to. It's close to where he lives. (He lives in Eagle Rock, the town next to ours. Gramma used to go there too, but she died two years ago.) Mama used to go there before she met Daddy. I heard that a bunch of stuck-up kids go there now. I've also heard that some of the church mothers look mean.

Grampa Edwards
(Mama's Daddy)

Stuck-up girl

Old church
mother

Just before we went to visit Eagle Rock on the first Sunday, Mama told me,

> Leslie, you know how important it is to respect your church leaders, like the pastor and the church mothers. Well, your dad and I have prayed about it. We don't agree with Pastor Samuels about some things. So we've decided to look for a new church.

✳ Me, trying to explain to Mama why I don't want to go to Eagle Rock. But she's giving me "the look."

I told Mama, "All my friends go to New Salem! What about choir and my drill team? I want to stay at New Salem!" As soon as I said that, Mama gave ME "the look." Then she said what she always says:

Sounds like somebody needs an attitude adjustment.

Daddy just stood there opening and closing his hand. I didn't want to laugh, because I knew why he did that. He's always saying stuff about being open to the changes God brings. "Can't go through life with a closed hand," he said. "You can't receive what God has that way."

It's not fair! We've been going to New Salem all my life. Nobody asked me what I want to do.

Ronnie is no help. He doesn't seem to care where we go to church. (And people say twins think alike.) RIGHT!

He makes friends easier than ~~Me~~ I do. And Tarita doesn't care about anything except her Barbie. (She can take that stupid doll wherever   she goes.)

So now I'll have to get used to a new church and a new, new pastor. Mama told me,

"God goes wherever you go. You don't have to be afraid of new

Tarita, my sister

Ronnie, my twi[n] brother

My Thoughts

If I were Leslie, this is how I would feel about having to change churches:

-Sad
- kind of upset
- afrid/taifide

Here are some words that describe how I usually deal with changes in my life:

- Hair die sad colen can't remove
- christmas when My elf disaperes

![open book icon]

My Verse

Jesus Christ is the same yesterday, today, and forever. Hebrews 13:8

Wow! No matter what happens in my life, I can count on one thing: Jesus never changes. I've gotta think about that. Let's see. Knowing that makes me feel . . .

Jesus Makes Me Love everyone Robers, pepol, animels, famliy and Me

My Prayer

Lord, I'm glad you never change! Help me deal with these changes that I'm going through right now: *Dear Lord help me with changeing My life and me Amen*

Amen.

June 6   A Walk on the Wild Side

Today I just felt like hangin' in my
room for a while after school. I LIKE MY
ROOM. Two months ago, I helped Daddy paint
the walls light green. Mama put up a white border
with purple and green flowers. I love green and purple.
They're my favorite colors. I'm wearing purple nail polish
right now! It's cool!

I call my room "Leslie's Lair." I thought that was a cool
name. I looked up the word _Lair_ in the dictionary
after hearing someone say it on TV. It means
"den or hideaway." It also means "resting
place." I like that last definition. It
reminds me of Psalm 23. We had to memo-
rize that at New Salem. I have a plaque
on the wall with the first two verses.

The LORD is my shepherd; I have everything I need. He lets me REST in green meadows; he leads me beside PEACEFUL streams.

Psalm 23:1-2

LESLIE'S LAIR—
I WANNA BE THERE
BECAUSE IT'S **WHERE**
I GO TO PREPARE

I know that last line doesn't make sense, but it's all I could think of that rhymes with where.

I always come here when I want to be by myself. Tarita tries to sneak into my lair sometimes. But she knows not to bug me when the door is closed. Sometimes she barges in, though. Wish I could lock the door!

When I look around my room, I see lots of pictures. There are pictures of my family, of course. But I have a lot of pictures from New Salem—my church family. On my dresser there's one of me with my BF 4E ❀ Vanessa Charles. Ronnie stuck his head in there. He's silly!

I'm keeping Spot in my room this week, since it's my turn. Spot's our goldfish. His bowl is on the dresser.

Vanessa and ~~me~~ I have been best friends since we were both three. She's 11 too. She'll be 12 before me, though. She was born in January, and I was born in March. March 23. She's always got my back. Her house is on Iroquois Avenue

BF 4E

❀ Best Friends 4 (for) Eternity

right behind ours. She's got my back and her house is out back!

I just wish her family would move to the new church too.

Or better still, I wish we would stay at New Salem.

IN ZACCHAEUS'S HOUSE
YOUTH SKIT 3 P.M.
Starring Leslie Larice Randalls
(Ha Ha Ha! I added this part after the play.)

New Salem is just like my room—it's like home to me. I can't help thinking of the fun we always had at church. On the wall kitty corner to my bed is a poster my friends and I made for a skit we did for Youth Sunday this spring. We had fun that day. I played one of the people who ate with Jesus at ~~Zacheus'~~ Zacchaeus's house. It was almost as fun as the skit we did for Black History month in the winter.

Just so I don't forget, the story of Zacchaeus is in Luke 19.

I just wish Mama and Daddy understood how much I want to stay at New Salem. I know everybody there! At Eagle Rock I only know Grampa.

God cares about
how you feel, Les.

Mama works as a grief counselor. She has an
office here at home. She helps people who
are sad. I just wish she realized how sad I
am to be leaving New Salem.
She says she does. But if she
knows how I feel, why aren't
we staying at New Salem?
Daddy told me that God cares about how I
feel. I just wish God would make Mama and
Daddy want to go back to New Salem.

When I told Vanessa about the move to Eagle Rock,
she left this message for me in my mailbox. We
sometimes send messages to each other in code.

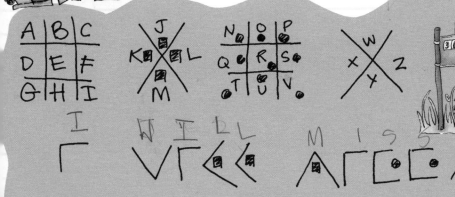

My Thoughts

Leslie's room tells me lots of things about her, like:

- she belives in Jesus
- she loves church

Here are some things that are in my room. I wonder what they tell people about me?

You belive in Jesus. You love atending church. You cares for others.

When I'm feeling sad I sometimes go to my room because . . . Jesus is There with you to make you happy and feel realy happy.

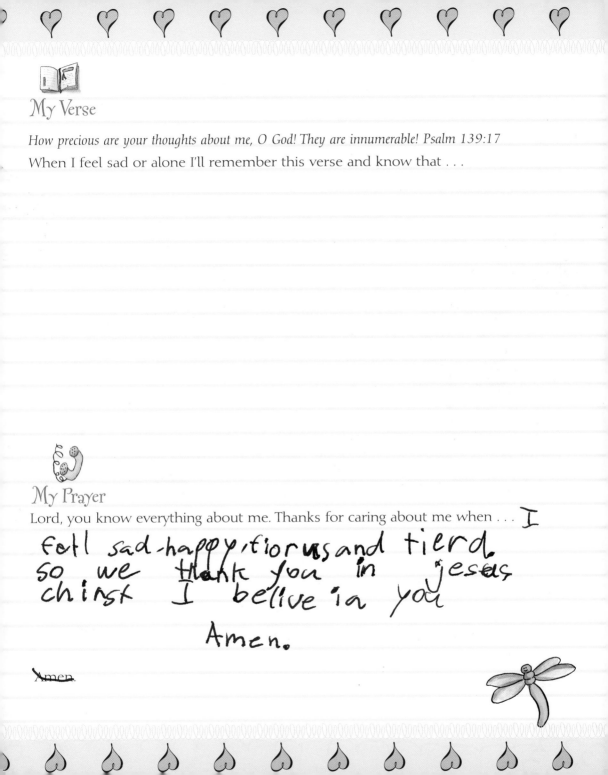

My Verse

How precious are your thoughts about me, O God! They are innumerable! Psalm 139:17

When I feel sad or alone I'll remember this verse and know that . . .

My Prayer

Lord, you know everything about me. Thanks for caring about me when . . . I fetl sad-happy,fiorus and tierd. so we thank you in jesas chinst I belive ia you

Amen.

Amen.

That Mean-a Regina

Well, we started at the new church today.

I was just glad that the air-conditioning worked. One time at New Salem it broke. Whooowee! It was H-O-T! Everybody was fanning themselves. Today I wore my new purple pants with the matching top that Mama finally let me buy with my own money. But when I got to Sunday school, I wished I hadn't worn my new outfit. Most of the girls in my class were dressed up.

I'm in the fifth and sixth grade girls' class. Eight girls came today. At my old church we only had about 4 or 5 kids who came regularly. Ronnie's in the fifth and sixth grade boys' class.

My Sunday school teacher is nice. Her name's Darlene. She's a college student. She goes to Hillside Park University. She made everybody introduce themselves. Some of the girls seemed nice. But four girls seemed really stuck-up—that's how I thought they would be.

They just talked to each other, and to one girl ~~especialy~~ especially—

Regina Lewis. I can already tell she thinks she's all that. When everyone introduced themselves, she just said

Hi

like she didn't really mean to be friendly. Then she started whispering to two of the girls who sat next to her. I wondered if they were talking about me.

For the rest of the class she sat there with her nose in the air. When Darlene started talking about how Christians are to be loving, I thought, "Well, that doesn't describe Regina."

Sunday school ends half an hour before church starts. Before church Mama had asked me if I wanted to go to children's church during the adult service. I wasn't going to go because I didn't know anybody hardly except Ronnie. So after Sunday school I went looking for Mama and Daddy. I had to go from the Sunday school building to the one next to it where the sanctuary is.

An old lady stopped me in the hall of the Sunday school building.

You look lost. Are you a visitor?

she asked.

I wanted to say,

I'm looking for my mama.

But I'd have felt like a little kid saying that. So I just kept walking.

The lady stopped me again.

Are you trying to find where
to go for children's church?
It's down the hall this way.

I shook my head, not really
wanting to go to children's church.
Since I didn't feel like talking, I went
into the women's washroom. After that I
went looking for Mama and Daddy. They were
both in the sanctuary talking to Grampa
AND THE LADY WHO STOPPED ME
IN THE HALL!
She smiled at me and then nudged my Grampa.

Is this your granddaughter, Luther?
How are you, young lady? I'm Mrs. Huff.
Welcome to Eagle Rock. We're glad
to have you here.

Hi   I said. Now that I think about it,
maybe I sounded like Regina.

My Thoughts

This is how Leslie felt about some of the people at the new church:

Darlene

Regina

Mrs. Huff

If I had been Leslie, I might not have noticed either, but she was welcomed by these people:

I wonder if I haven't always noticed when people are nice to me at *my* church. Hmmm. Maybe I can come up with a list of ways the people at my church show love to each other.

My Verse

Dear friends, let us continue to love one another, for love comes from God. Anyone who loves is born of God and knows God. 1 John 4:7

I guess I could plan how *I* can love my church family this week. This is what I'll do:

My Prayer

Lord, help me to be loving toward _____. Amen.

July 5 — Twice the Advice

FRIDAY ✽✽✽✽✽✽✽✽✽✽

I B-O-O-O-O-V-V-V-E summer and all. But some days there's just nothing to do. Today started out as a there's-nothing-to-do kind of day. I got up at 8. Tarita was already up watching her favorite show—The Cockadoodle Crunch Hour. That show is s-t-u-u-u-p-i-d! But I'm not supposed to tell Tarita that. Daddy doesn't like us to call anything stupid. We're supposed to watch what we say to each other. We're supposed to try to say positive things, instead of negative. SOMETIMES THAT'S HARD TO DO!

Daddy had already gone to work. He works in Chicago for an Internet software company. He usually leaves at 7 or 7:30. So he doesn't get to enjoy the summer at all! Ronnie was on the computer in the family room as usual, playing a game. Mama soon made him get off the computer and come eat breakfast. (She doesn't like him to be on the computer before breakfast. He's a computer hog.)

A VERSE WHEN I'M TEMPTED TO SAY THE WORST: Ephesians 4:29.

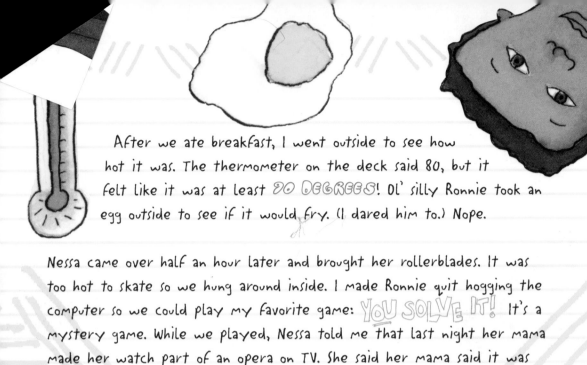

After we ate breakfast, I went outside to see how hot it was. The thermometer on the deck said 80, but it felt like it was at least 90 DEGREES! Ol' silly Ronnie took an egg outside to see if it would fry. (I dared him to.) Nope.

Nessa came over half an hour later and brought her rollerblades. It was too hot to skate so we hung around inside. I made Ronnie quit hogging the computer so we could play my favorite game: YOU SOLVE IT! It's a mystery game. While we played, Nessa told me that last night her mama made her watch part of an opera on TV. She said her mama said it was educational. So we sang pop songs we like in opera lady voices. We just wanted to see what they would sound like. THAT WAS SO FUNNY! That's when Mama came in and asked if we didn't have anything better to do.

When I told Mama that we didn't have anything to do, she said she had a surprise for us. She didn't have any clients scheduled today. So she and Auntie Sharda had decided to take us—me and Ronnie and Tarita and our cousin Lance— to Splash-tastic Water Park! Mama said Vanessa could come too. Yay!

LA LA LA LA LA

I wore the purple, green, and blue suit I got last year. (Mama wouldn't get me a new one for this summer.) Nessa's suit has the same flowered pattern, except hers is ~~fushia~~ fuchsia pink, blue, and green.

Before we left, Mama braided my hair and Tarita's. Then we piled in the van and drove over to Auntie Sharda's to pick up her and Lance. Auntie Sharda is ~~Daddy's~~ older sister. But she's only a year older, just like Lance is only a year older than ~~me and Ronnie~~ Ronnie and me. I always laugh when we drive over to their house. They only live two blocks away! They could've walked over to our house!

Lance's Dog,
Freedom

Just as we were leaving, their dog tried to escape out of the yard. FREEDOM is the perfect name for that golden retriever. She loves her freedom. Auntie Sharda yelled at Lance for not closing the gate all the way. We all laughed at that. Lance is forever getting into trouble for something.

We had to drive forever and ever and ever—for a whole hour to North River. That's a town several miles north of Chicago. (Our town is south of Chicago.)

Lance,
our cousin

I B-O-O-O-V-V-V-E Splash-tastic Water Park, even though it's usually c-r-o-w-w-d-e-d! My favorite part is the slide where two people can go down on tubes at the same time. B-O-O-O-O-O-O-B! At the park, Ronnie and Lance tried to get me to go down the BIG slide. There was no way I was going down that slide! You're way up in the air, maybe 70 or 80 feet or so! And you go zooming down way too fast! I'm not crazy!

Nessa and me Nessa and I went down the 2-Tube Slide a bunch of times. Then Mama wanted Ronnie and me to take turns taking Tarita on the kiddie slide. She wanted to go off and gab with Auntie Sharda!

While Ness, Lance, and I were floating along in our tubes soaking up some rays, Lance asked me how I liked Eagle Rock. He would have to bring that up! I splashed him good! After that I told them how hard it was to make friends because some of the kids act stuck-up. That's when Nessa and Lance started giving me advice.

I changed the subject after that because I suddenly remembered what Daddy said about watching my words. Hmmm. Maybe I don't always do that when it comes to talking about Eagle Rock.

If they try to diss you, diss 'em and run!

Girl, give 'em a chance! You've only been there a few weeks. Maybe they're not all stuck-up.

My Thoughts

If I were Leslie, would I follow Vanessa's advice or Lance's? I guess this is what I'd do:

Come to think of it, the advice Leslie's father gave her about watching her words is pretty good because . . .

My Verse

Let us consider how we may spur one another on toward love and good deeds. Hebrews 10:24

Let's see. I know that "spurring" someone on toward "good deeds" means to encourage that person to do good. I'm going to make a list of the people from Leslie's story. Then I'm going to put a check beside the name of each person who encouraged Leslie to do good.

Here are some ways that I can spur someone on to do good:

My Prayer

Lord, most times I think I try to encourage my friends. Do I discourage them sometimes? I don't mean to. Help me to "spur on" my friend

_____ this week to do this:

Amen.

July 14   Click with a Clique?

One more Sunday down at Eagle Rock. I marked it off on the calendar.

I didn't want to go at first. At breakfast I told Mama that my stomach hurt. Well, it did sort of, but not much.

As soon as I said that, I could tell Ronnie was grinning at me even before I looked at him.

Nosy Tarita said,

Mama, are you going to let Leslie stay home?

Nobody asked her!

Mama had her "You're going" face on. I think she knew I was faking it. Daddy just looked at me and shook his head.

At least one good thing happened: I wore my new blue-jean skirt and my favorite short-sleeved top.

Regina and her friends. I think their names are

Tamran Kalli Ashley

For a church that's supposed to be so friendly, hardly anybody acts that friendly at Eagle Rock. ✳ Regina and her friends act like they only want to be friends with each other. They're all in my class. They seem the most stuck-up of all. The other girls in my class seem OK. But hardly any of them said anything to me today.

Nicki sat next to me in Sunday school and at least said hi. I was glad that I remembered her name. She seems kind of quiet. She didn't open her mouth to answer any of Darlene's questions.

Hi

Nicki

After church Mama kept telling me I need to join some of the youth activities at church.

There are a lot of activities for kids here at Eagle Rock. A lot more than we had at New Salem. And I just know my daughter would love to join the choir. Right, sweetie?

I wanted to ignore what Mama said. But I can't ignore her for too long. She won't let me! Anyway, she knows I love to sing. But I don't want to join the choir! I don't even want to be at this church! I want to go back to New Salem.

As we left church I asked Daddy,

Why can't we go back?

We've been through this already. Give Eagle Rock a chance, OK?

Daddy waved his open hand toward me. I rolled my eyes.

Nobody talks to me. Well . . . one girl did.

To be a friend you've got to act like a friend. It beats complaining.

Daddy finally got through to me when he said,

Instead of complaining, I wish my girl would pray.

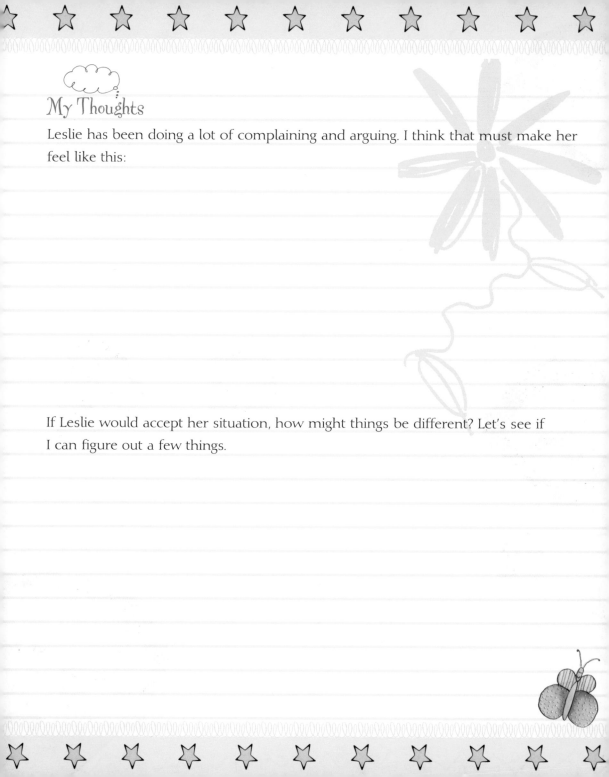

My Thoughts

Leslie has been doing a lot of complaining and arguing. I think that must make her feel like this:

If Leslie would accept her situation, how might things be different? Let's see if I can figure out a few things.

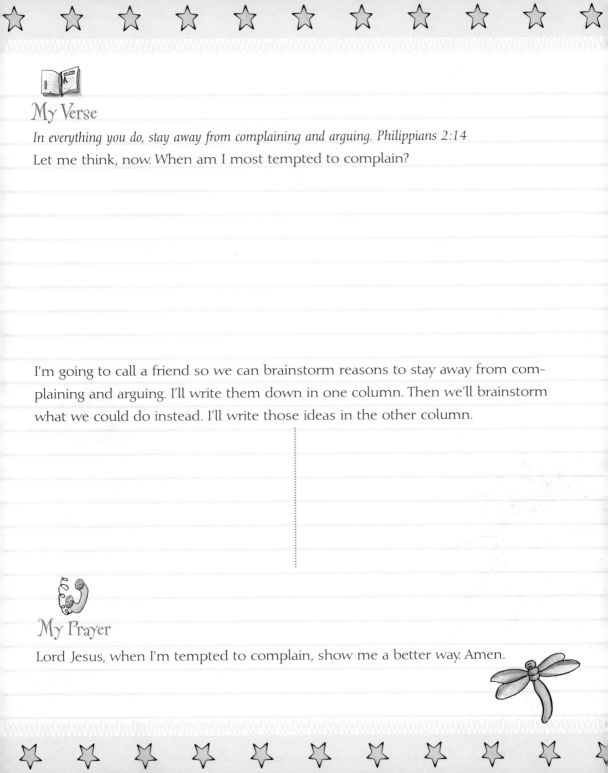

My Verse

In everything you do, stay away from complaining and arguing. Philippians 2:14

Let me think, now. When am I most tempted to complain?

I'm going to call a friend so we can brainstorm reasons to stay away from complaining and arguing. I'll write them down in one column. Then we'll brainstorm what we could do instead. I'll write those ideas in the other column.

My Prayer

Lord Jesus, when I'm tempted to complain, show me a better way. Amen.

Which Way to Play?

It's just July and hot enough to fry!

It's been a SUMMER NUMMER BUMMER LUMMER kind of Saturday. There's too much to do. And everything's happening at 3 p.m. today. In two hours.

Decisions. Decisions. What to do? What to do? New Salem's having a movie afternoon for the youth. But at Eagle Rock, the fifth and sixth grade girls' and boys' classes are going skating at a rink here in Hillside Park. Darlene called at 9:30 this morning to remind me about it. I would love to go skating. I know Mama would drive me. She's been asking me and asking me if I want to go. I've thought about it. But I'm scared to go by myself. I don't know that many people at Eagle Rock. We've only been there a month and a half! Even Ronnie's not going. He's got park district soccer this afternoon.

They're showing God's Open Door. There's gonna be popcorn!

Nessa's the one who told me about the movie. I've seen that video before. So I asked Nessa if she wouldn't rather go skating.

C'mon, Ness! Let's go skating! Pleez go?

But she couldn't go. Her mother absolutely positively said no. I heard her saying it when Vanessa put down the phone and went to ask her. Mostly, she said she ABSOLUTELY (she always uses that word) would not give Vanessa another cent  to spend on anything else. So Nessa came back and said that she and Halle Hernandez, Alexis Johnson, Ruth Dinkins, and K. K. Stewart were going to be at the church for sure. Nessa, Halle, and ~~me~~ I are tight. I like Alexis, Ruth, and K. K. too. They were all in my Sunday school class when I was at New Salem. We did a lot of things together. BUT IF I STOP GOING TO STUFF AT NEW SALEM, WILL THEY STILL BE MY FRIENDS?

I waited until Mama's office hours were over to ask her what she thought. She had a funny look on her face when she told me,

Leslie, you have to decide for yourself what you want to do. You're old enough now.

I thought for sure she'd try to talk me into going skating at Eagle Rock. All this time I've been wishing that Mama would let me choose what I want to do. Now I wish she would've decided for me.

Maybe I'll list what's good and what's bad about going to either place. Daddy once said that he does that when he has to make a decision. He always says I should pray too. But I think I'll make the list first, then pray.

GOOD

NEW SALEM MOVIE AFTERNOON
- I'd be with my friends.

EAGLE ROCK SKATING
- Skating is really, really fun.
- Darlene will be there.

BAD

NEW SALEM MOVIE AFTERNOON
- I've seen the video.

EAGLE ROCK SKATING
- I don't know that many people.
- My friends won't be there.
- I'm not that good at skating backwards. I might fall on my face.
- Ronnie's not going.

I wonder if Nicki's going skating. She's nice. And so are Aubrei and Reesa. If I knew their phone numbers, I'd ask. But since I don't know if Nicki or anybody else good is going, I have to add that to the <u>Bad</u> List.

GOOD

NEW SALEM MOVIE AFTERNOON
- I'd be with my friends.

EAGLE ROCK SKATING
- Skating is really, really fun.
- Darlene will be there.

BAD

NEW SALEM MOVIE AFTERNOON
- I've seen the video.

EAGLE ROCK SKATING
- I don't know that many people.
- My friends won't be there.
- I'm not that good at skating backwards. I might fall on my face.
- Ronnie's not going.
- Nicki may not be there.

The way I see it, the skating thing has more bad points than good. I guess that means I shouldn't go to the skating party.

Sure would've been fun to go skating. Oh well. I'll still pray about it. But I think I already know the answer.

Wish we could go back to Splash-tastic Water Park, where we went a few weeks ago!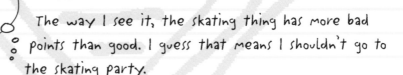

My Thoughts

I think Leslie was afraid to go skating because . . .

The way I see it, Leslie didn't want to miss out on the movie because . . .

If I were Leslie, on Saturday afternoon I would go _____
because . . .

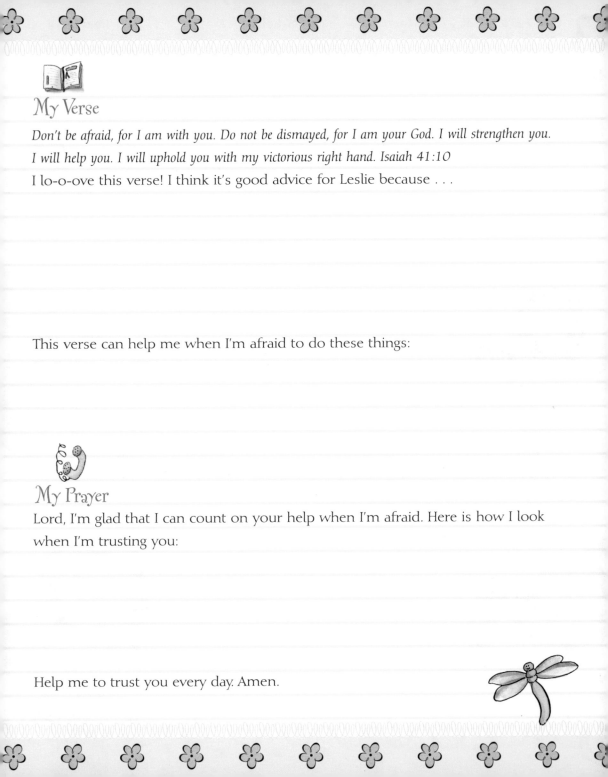

My Verse

Don't be afraid, for I am with you. Do not be dismayed, for I am your God. I will strengthen you. I will help you. I will uphold you with my victorious right hand. Isaiah 41:10

I lo-o-ove this verse! I think it's good advice for Leslie because . . .

This verse can help me when I'm afraid to do these things:

My Prayer

Lord, I'm glad that I can count on your help when I'm afraid. Here is how I look when I'm trusting you:

Help me to trust you every day. Amen.

August 4

Trouble with Tarita

Having a six-year-old sister can be a real pain sometimes. I try to tell Mama that, but she tells me to be thankful that I have a sister. O-o-o-o-o!

LITTLE SISTERS ARE LIKE AN ANNOYING FLEA BITE! THAT DOESN'T RHYME ALL THE WAY, BUT WHAT ELSE CAN I SAY?

Tarita is always trying to hang with me. She tries to follow me around even though she has friends of her own!

Sometimes I don't mind it. But sometimes I do. That's why I'm glad I have this journal to write in. I can say what I want about anyone! I can say:

TARITA GETS ON MY NERVES SOMETIMES!

Like today. She kept after me to play Barbies with her after church. I didn't feel like it. All I wanted to do was enjoy the video that Ronnie and I were trying to watch in the family room downstairs. So that was when she asked me

> How come you don't want to be friends with anybody at church?

THAT GOT MY ATTENTION. I didn't want to act like I cared, but I still wanted to know where she got that idea.

> See, the way to handle Tarita is to act like you don't care what she has to say.

Ronnie taught me that. When you look like you're dying to know what she knows, Tarita will laugh and run off, like she's so proud that she has information you want. So I went back to watching the video like she wasn't even there. After about five minutes Tarita goes,

> Two big girls were talking after Sunday school. They said you act like you don't want to be friends with anybody.

> Tarita calls anybody older than her a "big girl."

That was exactly what I thought about Regina and her friends! I suddenly felt like crying. I started asking Tarita questions like, "You heard that today? What two girls?" before I could stop myself. I COULDN'T BELIEVE I WAS TRYING TO GET INFORMATION FROM MY SIX-YEAR-OLD SISTER!

Then Ronnie said

> You believe Tarita heard that? Even if she did, you know it ain't true.

I didn't know what to think. Mama came downstairs at that point carrying a load of clothes. I had just been wondering how much

Mama had overheard when I heard her scold Tarita about repeating gossip. MAMA HATES GOSSIP.

After that I got up and went to my room. I didn't even care if I saw the rest of the video. I needed to be by myself.

As soon as I closed the door to my room, I remembered I could pray. I knew that was God's reminder to chill and talk to him. So I did. I told him how upset I was about what Tarita overheard. In the middle of the prayer, I heard a knock at my door. Tarita started begging to come in. I told her to go away. Then she told me she was sorry. Pretty soon I heard her go down the hall.

I felt bad then. It wasn't Tarita's fault that those girls said what they did. As soon as I started praying again, I knew I should tell Tarita that I was sorry too.

Before I did, I thought about what a lady at

church (Mrs. Huff) said today.

Maybe that was God's way of letting me know that what those girls said wasn't true (and that I should tell Tarita I'm sorry). I hate when people think things about me that aren't true. I know I didn't want our family to come to the Eagle Rock church. But that doesn't mean I don't want to be friends with anyone there.

> You seem like a nice young lady.

> Nicki's not like Regina and her friends. Maybe we can be friends.

It's funny. Today I almost felt OK about being at Eagle Rock. In Sunday school, we got into a good discussion. We talked about school and how hard it can be sometimes. (SCHOOL STARTS AT THE END OF THIS MONTH! UGH!) I found out that Regina and her friends Tamran and Ashley will go to Lambert Academy. I should've known Regina would go to an expensive school like that. Then we talked about our families. I said something funny about Tarita and how she always wants me to play Barbies with her. Everyone laughed. Even Regina.

Now I'm wondering which of them could have said what Tarita overheard. I don't think Nicki would have said that. Was it Regina? Tamran? (I think she's Regina's best friend.) Kalli? Brianna? Ashley? Claudette? Aubrei? Reesa?

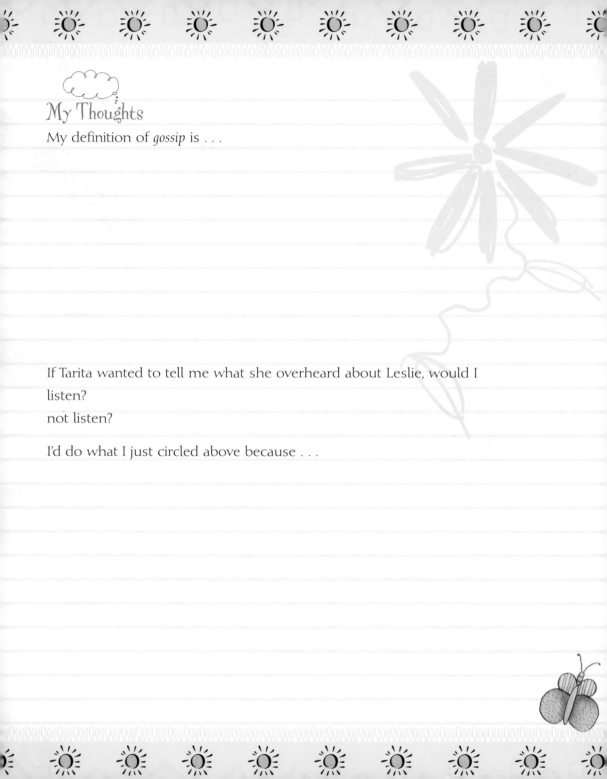

My Thoughts

My definition of *gossip* is . . .

If Tarita wanted to tell me what she overheard about Leslie, would I listen?

not listen?

I'd do what I just circled above because . . .

My Verse

Without wood a fire goes out; without gossip a quarrel dies down. Proverbs 26:20

Hmm. Two girls gossiped about Leslie, and Tarita gossiped about what they said. All that gossip kept Leslie and the others from being friends just like more wood on a fire keeps the fire from going out. So this is what I'll try to do when I hear gossip:

I'll draw a picture to help me remember Proverbs 26:20 and to help me remember not to gossip:

My Prayer

Father God, I need your help not to listen when I hear gossip and I'm tempted to repeat it. Amen.

August 14 — Do Clothes Make the Christian?

Today (Wednesday) Mama drove Nessa, Halle, and me to the mall to go to the movies. Mama gave me money to buy popcorn and a Coke, then told us to meet her in the food court at 3:30—a whole hour and a half after the movie. Finally Mama is letting me do more things with my friends. I guess she sees that I'm growing up! After all, I'll be a 6ᵀᴴ grader in TWO WEEKS! I can hardly believe school starts then!!

This has been a good summer. I hate to see it end. ~~Me and Nessa~~ Nessa and I just chilled around the 'hood mostly. Halle got to go to summer camp for a week. She just came back yesterday. I've been to camp once, but not this summer.

The movie was G-O-O-O-O-O-O-O-O-O-D! It was called MYSTERY AT THE LAKE. I love mysteries! I like to see if I can solve the mystery before the end. This one was about a summer camp. Some of the kids at the camp were having trouble fitting in. (That's how I still feel at Eagle Rock Bible Church.) The kids in the movie were accused of stealing some valuable camp equipment. I guessed who the real thieves were before the end of the movie. Halle and Nessa were still stumped. Ha!

After the movie we stopped at our favorite store—Nina's Casual Closet—to look at clothes. It's on the second floor of the mall. That store has some* fly stuff. A lot of it is expensive, though.

ME, all grown up! No wonder I can't fit in! Ha Ha Ha!

*FLY = COOL

We all tried on clothes, even though we had
no money to buy anything. Nessa said she
wanted to look at some stuff for school. Halle tried on a
cool red-and-white striped, long-sleeved T-shirt and a
blue-jean skort. I tried on a skort too. Skorts are good if
you suddenly get the urge to turn a cartwheel.✳ Ness
tried on a pair of overall shorts on sale. She won't wear a skirt or
anything that looks like one if she can help it, but she tried on a red dress
just for laughs. It's totally NOT Nessa.

In the dressing room we put on a mini-fashion show, trading clothes
back and forth. That was fun.

When we went to look for more clothes to put on, I
saw the ~~fushia~~ fuchsia and yellow dress that Regina Lewis
wore to church one Sunday. It was on a rack with other
GESTURES outfits. I showed it to Ness and Halle. Nessa thought
it was ugly. But Halle liked it. I could tell that when she said,
"Bonita!" I know what that word means in Spanish: pretty.
(Halle's trying to help us learn Spanish.) I thought the dress was
pretty too, but it's not something I would wear.

✳ This is an
example
of a time
when a
skort would
be perfect!

All the kids in the 'hood want JESTURES stuff. Their stuff is all the way fly. When I was in the store with Mama two months ago, I begged her to buy me a JESTURES shirt. She looked at the price tag and said,

> Girl, you must be kidding.

I knew there was no way to talk her into it. (Maybe I'll work on Grandmama Randalls, Daddy's mother.)

I told Nessa and Halle that Regina's parents must buy her expensive clothes, because she always seems to wear something from JESTURES or KiDZAzZ. That's another expensive clothes (clothing?) store at the mall. Her friends wear clothes like that too. I think Regina's family's got mucho money. (Dinero, as Halle would say.) Maybe her friends' families do too.

Mama always says I think about clothes too much. She says wearing expensive clothes doesn't make a person better than anyone else. Maybe she's right. Just last Sunday Pastor Wallace talked about how God accepts everyone. He doesn't care what we look like or how we dress. That sounded nice. Then Pastor said,

> Come as you are to Eagle Rock.

I guess that means people can dress any way they want when they go to church. But I feel kinda like I'm not dressed ~~good~~ well enough when I see the different kinds of really nice clothes some of the people at Eagle Rock wear.

Three weeks ago I heard two girls from the seventh and eighth grade class talking about another girl because they didn't like her outfit. One girl said, "She probably shops at Waltons." That's a discount store in Hillside Park. What they said got me thinking. Mama always gets our clothes on sale. Sometimes she shops at Waltons. She'll probably want to go there to shop for my school clothes. I do like most of the clothes I wear. I REALLY like the outfits that Mama lets me pick out for myself. But I don't know if they're good enough for Eagle Rock.

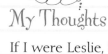

My Thoughts

If I were Leslie, this is how I'd feel about getting all expensive, name-brand clothes like Jestures and Kidzazz, the way Regina does:

This is what I think is important about clothes:

My Verse

The Lord doesn't make decisions the way you do! People judge by outward appearance, but the Lord looks at a person's thoughts and intentions. 1 Samuel 16:7

I'm glad this verse is in the Bible. It tells me that the *inside* of a person matters most to God. I think that's because . . .

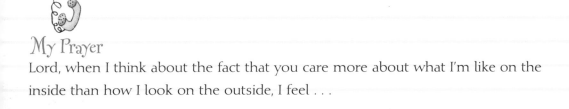

My Prayer

Lord, when I think about the fact that you care more about what I'm like on the inside than how I look on the outside, I feel . . .

Thanks, God! Amen.

Darlene called me on Wednesday this week. She said she's praying for me. She's so nic

August 18 — A Friend Indeed

Today in Sunday school it was "Regina this" and "Regina that." When Darlene asked us how our week was, Regina had to brag about her family's trip to Disney World. BIG WHOOP. Then she made sure EVERYbody, their grandmother, and the state of Texas knew that she and her friends had been asked to join the youth choir. I rolled my eyes when she said that. I thought we couldn't go to youth church until we were in the 6TH grade. Sixth grade hasn't <u>started</u> yet. I guess Regina and her friends can go because Regina's father is one of the deacons. Maybe her friends' fathers are too.

Three Sundays in AUGUST gone already.

I can almost hear Mama now:

Somebody's grumbling.

Maybe I am. (I'm sorry, God!) But nobody invited <u>me</u> to join the youth choir. And I like to sing! ♪ ♪ ♫ ♫ 𝄢

At least I got one invitation. Nicki invited me to go with her family for ice cream after church. Mama and Daddy instantly said yes when I asked. I think they were glad that Nicki invited me. Mama squeezed my shoulder as I left to go with Nicki's family.

Wanna go with me and my family for ice cream after church?

yes

Tarita begged to go too. I was afraid Mama and Daddy would let her, even though Nicki just asked _me_ to go. But they didn't!

no

BARNETT'S
The cream of the
CREAM

We went to Barnett's Ice Cream Shop—my favorite place for ice cream. There's one in Hillside Park. Everybody goes there.

The place was packed since today was s-o-o-o-o-o hot—over 85 degrees! I couldn't wait to get inside and get some cool ice cream. I ordered my favorite—a scoop of banana and a scoop of chocolate-chip fudge with caramel sauce. YUM-M-M.

Nicki's family seems nice. She's got a little brother (Evan) who's seven and a sister (Rachel) who's eight. Rachel is quiet like Nicki. Evan is the talker of the family. He's always telling jokes the way Tarita does. (Neither one of them can tell a joke.)

Mr. Phillips talked to me like I was a person, not just a kid. He asked me how I liked being at Eagle Rock Bible Church. I just said

It's OK.

Nicki told me that her father teaches physics at the high school in my town—Hill Park High. (I don't know why the high school isn't called Hillside Park like the town and the

college.) Mr. Phillips doesn't seem like a nerd, though. Mrs. Phillips is a lawyer. She seems quiet like Nicki does.

While we were there, I asked Nicki why I hardly ever see her at children's church. (I've only gone twice so far. But that's where we're supposed to go until we're in sixth grade and we can go to youth church.) Nicki looked embarrassed like it was hard for her to say why. Then Mrs. Phillips said she was trying to get Nicki to go.

Some friends of Nicki's parents came in, so Mr. and Mrs. Phillips started talking to them. That's when Nicki told me that her family has only been at Eagle Rock for a year. It's been hard for her to make friends too. She said she prayed and asked God for a friend. I guess I was an answer to prayer. That made me feel good. It's cool to finally have a friend at church. Vanessa was my best friend 4 eternity at home, at school, and at church. Now she's just my BF 4E at home and at school. I miss being at church with her.

Nicki's not like Vanessa. Nessa talks and talks and talks. We can talk about anything and everything for hours.

Blah Blah Blah Blah Blah Blah Blah

Nessa and I like the same kind of music (RAP, R&B) and the same shows and everything. Nicki is quiet and seems very shy. It's hard to get any information out of her. I don't know what music groups or TV

Les, if you really want to get to know somebody, you need to ask them questions.

shows she likes. I know she goes to Eagle Rock Elementary. At least she's tried to be friendly to me (unlike Regina and her friends; they still barely say anything to me). Maybe I need to ask her more questions. Daddy told me that's the way to learn about people.

When I got home I told God, "THANKS FOR TODAY." Then I called Vanessa. Daddy kept saying, "Ten minutes! Ten minutes!" I'm allowed to talk just ten minutes on the phone to Vanessa these days. Daddy says I talk too much. (I don't know why he thinks that. I don't talk as much as Vanessa does.) I told Vanessa about Nicki. Vanessa said that Nicki seems nice. Maybe one day she'll get to meet Nicki.

Then Vanessa started telling me what's going on at New Salem. I was glad I had to get off the phone then. I didn't want to hear what's going on. I knew I'd start missing my friends at New Salem all over again.

Blah Blah Blah Blah Blah Blah

My Thoughts

Leslie's day was groovy because . . .

Yet there were some not-so-groovy things about her day. Things like . . .

A groovy day for me involves these activities:

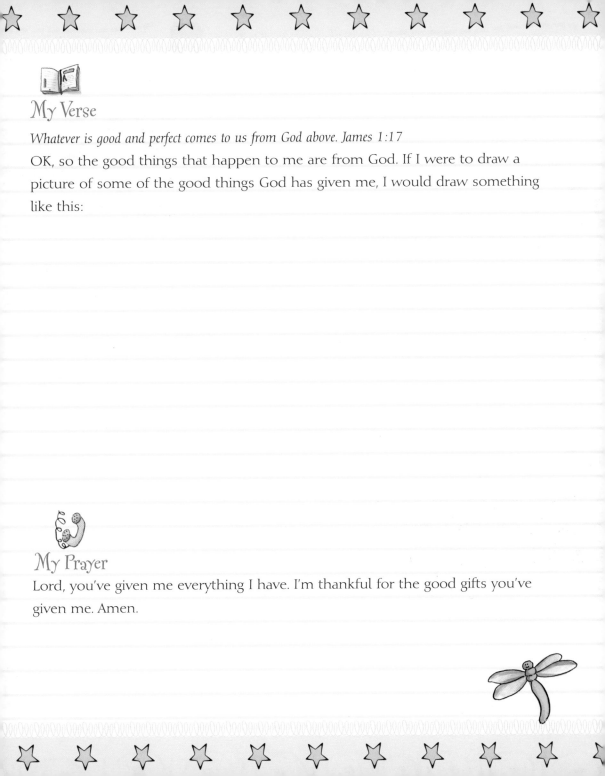

My Verse

Whatever is good and perfect comes to us from God above. James 1:17

OK, so the good things that happen to me are from God. If I were to draw a picture of some of the good things God has given me, I would draw something like this:

My Prayer

Lord, you've given me everything I have. I'm thankful for the good gifts you've given me. Amen.

End of summer vacation

August 22 — Bike Hike

Today Nessa and I went on our annual right-before-school bike hike around the 'hood. We've done this since we were in third grade. It's sort of like a good-bye to summer kind of thing. It's so hard to believe that school starts NEXT WEEK. 6TH grade!!!!!!!!!!!

I l-o-o-o-o-o-v-v-v-e to ride my bike. It's purple and black and is TOO COOL TO FOOL. (Ronnie says that. He's silly.) It's midnight cool. (That's what Nessa and I call something that is REALLY, REALLY COOL. Cool to the tenth power cool.)

My bike SO COOL IT RULES!

COOL¹⁰

Nessa's is red and gold. She loves red.

The weather was perfect today for a bike ride. It was probably 70 something.

Back when we were in third grade, we couldn't go very far. Come to think of it, we still can't go too far. We start at Nessa's house and go down Willowbrook to McKinley, past Archer over to St. James, then up St. James to Arapaho, where New Salem is.

Nessa's bike

It was weird being so close to New Salem and knowing I don't go there anymore.

I asked Nessa about Halle. She said Halle wasn't at church last Sunday. Then I asked her about our Sunday school teacher, Mrs. Jones. (Well, I guess she's just Vanessa's teacher now, not mine.) She said Mrs. Jones was sick last week. Then she told me that Vida doesn't go to the church anymore. That shocked me! Vida was one of the youth leaders. She was nice. Vanessa isn't sure who will take her place.

Good old New Salem. I sure miss being there. But what's funny is . . . it doesn't hurt as much as it used to. I guess that's because I still get to see some of the kids who go there (except for Ruth). Even so, I wish my family was still there.

Then Nessa asked me what's going on at Eagle Rock. I told her I didn't really know. Nothing, I guess. After we rode past New Salem a couple of times, we decided that we needed some ice cream. So we rode down Arapaho to Archer, then took Archer over to my house. I knew Mama wouldn't let me buy anything from the ice cream man since we have ice cream bars in the freezer. Me and Nessa and I took a couple of those and hung out in the family room. It's always nice and cool down there.

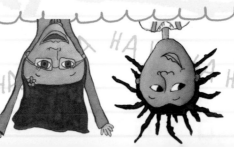

Me and Nessa
Nessa and me

hangin' out

HA HA HA HA HA HA HA HA HA HA

We changed our minds. We're going to New Salem.

Just as Nessa started telling me some other stuff about New Salem, Mama came out of her office. (I guess she had finished her office hours.) She asked Vanessa about some of the people who go to New Salem. I kind of hoped she'd suddenly say that she and Daddy changed their minds and that we'd be going back to New Salem. But then she invited Vanessa to visit our new church!

After Vanessa left, I tried to remind Mama about New Salem by telling her some of the other things Nessa said. But Mama just gave me "the look" and asked me what was going on with the kids in my Sunday school class at Eagle Rock. I told her I didn't know. Then she gave me another look. I gave her my "What, Mama?" look.

Body of Christ

Mama's always after me to be concerned about others, especially the people at church. I tried to explain to her that I'm showing concern for the body of Christ. Can I help it if the part of the body I'm concerned about is New Salem?

My Thoughts

Hmm. I can tell that Leslie is most concerned about these people:

I think Leslie's mother asked her about the kids at Eagle Rock for this reason:

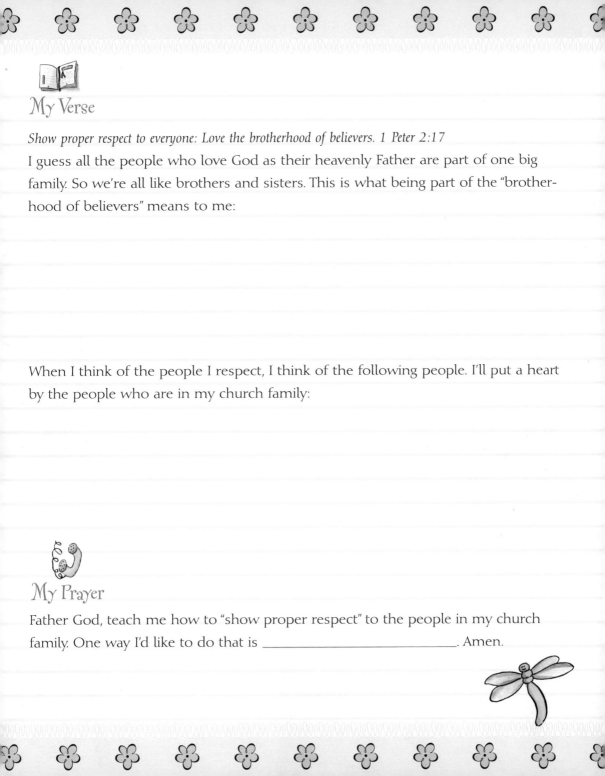

My Verse

Show proper respect to everyone: Love the brotherhood of believers. 1 Peter 2:17

I guess all the people who love God as their heavenly Father are part of one big family. So we're all like brothers and sisters. This is what being part of the "brother-hood of believers" means to me:

When I think of the people I respect, I think of the following people. I'll put a heart by the people who are in my church family:

My Prayer

Father God, teach me how to "show proper respect" to the people in my church family. One way I'd like to do that is _____. Amen.

August 25: It's (Mostly) All Good

It's Sunday night. I've got to say that this weekend has been G-O-O-O-O-O GOOD. All the way good! Well, mostly all good. On Saturday I found $2 on the ground near the mailbox on the corner of our street. That afternoon some of Tarita's friends came over for a play date Mama had set up. So Tarita had someone else to play Barbies with her. YES-S-S! And Saturday night we had pizza from Avellino's—my favorite!

cha-ching!

This morning Darlene was sick, :(so Mrs. Huff was our Sunday school teacher. At first I thought <u>Mrs. Huff</u> was sick when she walked into the room where we have Sunday school. She seemed to be huffing and puffing. But she said she was OK. She brought brownies to class! Yummy!

We had a small class today. Only five of us showed up. So we didn't divide into discussion groups like we usually do. Regina was there, but the girls she's buddy-buddy with (Tamran and Kalli) weren't there. I thought I would drop dead on the floor with shock when she said hi to me today. I guess she said that because none of her friends were around. "Hi" was all she said, though.

CRASH!

Hi

HA HA HA   HA HA   HA HA HA

Would a breath of air from Mrs. Huff be a *HUFF PUFF*? Ronnie told me that one.

For some reason I was the center of attention in Sunday school. Reesa asked me what having a twin is like. Everybody looked interested. (Everybody but Regina, that is.) So I told them that Ronnie and I are alike in some ways and different in others. (For real!) He loves basketball and golf. I can take sports or leave 'em.

YUK!

But we're tight. I think we think the same way about a lot of things. We both hate black licorice and coconut.*

Then Mrs. Huff asked us if we're part of the Church Pen Pal Exchange. If not, she will make sure that those of us who want them will receive pen pals. Kids in different churches across the country can sign up to be pen pals. That's something they didn't do at New Salem. I have a pen pal. I've written to her twice already. Her name is Melissa Frink. It'll be fun to get to know her. She'll be in 6TH grade just like me. She lives in Maple Lanes. That's about 25 miles from Hillside Park.

Maple Lanes

After class today Reesa gave Nicki and me an invitation to a sleep-over at her house next weekend. I didn't see her give Regina one.

What a good weekend.

My Thoughts

I think this weekend was mostly all good for Leslie because she felt accepted by others. Here are some of the ways that others showed they accepted her:

If I were Leslie, I would do or say this to help others accept me:

Here is one way that Leslie could show her acceptance of others:

My Verse

Accept each other just as Christ has accepted you; then God will be glorified. Romans 15:7

Wow! Jesus Christ, God's very own Son, accepts ME! Whenever I think of that, I feel like this:

Whenever I accept others, this is how God must feel:

My Prayer

Lord, please show me how to love and accept others the way that you love and accept me. I especially want your help to accept _____.

September 1

A Huff Gone in a Puff?

It's the first Sunday in September. It's still AUGUST hot, though.

I ate all I could and then I felt all blown up!

Today after church our family and Nicki's family went out to eat at the HILLSIDE PARK BUFFET. That's an all-you-can-eat place. It was Grampa's idea. He said we should have a back-to-school celebration. Yeah, right! Mama and Daddy laughed. Then Daddy acted as if he was cracking a joke by saying that all parents should celebrate when the kids go back to school. Mr. and Mrs. Phillips laughed, but Ronnie, Nicki, and I just looked at each other. That wasn't funny.

I'm really glad that Nicki and I are friends.

Everyone kept asking us about school. How do you like school? Who is your teacher? I DIDN'T WANT TO TALK ABOUT SCHOOL. So I just said, "Mr. Spivak" (my teacher) and "It's OK."

Then Grampa said what he usually says when this time of year comes:

> Be thankful you can get an education.
> Many people wish they had one. Blah. Blah. Blah.

I whispered to Nicki that I wished she went to my school. I only see her on Sundays. We sit together in youth church. (Now that sixth grade has ~~oficially~~ officially started, we've moved up from children's church.) After that I suddenly started paying attention to what the grown-ups were talking about. Grampa said that the pastor got a call this week about Mrs. Huff. She was sick for a while with a bad summer cold that turned into the flu. She had to go to the hospital for a while. Now she has to stay home and rest. Grampa wonders who will be in charge of the after-school tutoring program at church. (I guess Mrs. Huff ran that program. I didn't know.) Gramma Edwards died of a stroke two years ago. So I only have one grandmother—Grandmama Randalls. She lives way-y-y-y-y down in Houston, Texas. I always call her Grandmama. When my other grandmother was alive, I called her Gramma.

I got scared all of a sudden, like when I first learned Gramma was sick. I sort of remember not seeing Mrs. Huff at church today. She didn't seem all that well last week. It's funny how I didn't notice her

much before. I kind of just thought she'd always be there like the carpet and pews and stuff.

I asked Grampa if he thought she'd be all right. He said yes and that he planned to visit her. I felt better. I guess I didn't realize how much I liked Mrs. Huff. She's one of the nicest of the church mothers. Some of the others seem grumpy sometimes. I don't think I ever told her thanks for the nice things she's said about me or brought to me. She was the first person to help me feel welcome in the church.

All the way home from the restaurant I thought about what I could do for Mrs. Huff. I thought maybe I could bake her some get-well chocolate chip cookies. Maybe I could send her a card too. Yeah. That's what I'll do.

This is what Ness sent me from a Web site she found for Christian kids. You're supposed to color the shapes and then look at the part you didn't color and you'll discover a fruit of the Spirit. It's cool. Maybe Mrs. Huff would like it too.

My Thoughts

To me Leslie seems to show thankfulness to God when she thinks of these people:

She shows her thankfulness by doing these good things:

My Verse

Whenever we have the opportunity, we should do good to everyone, especially to our Christian brothers and sisters. Galatians 6:10

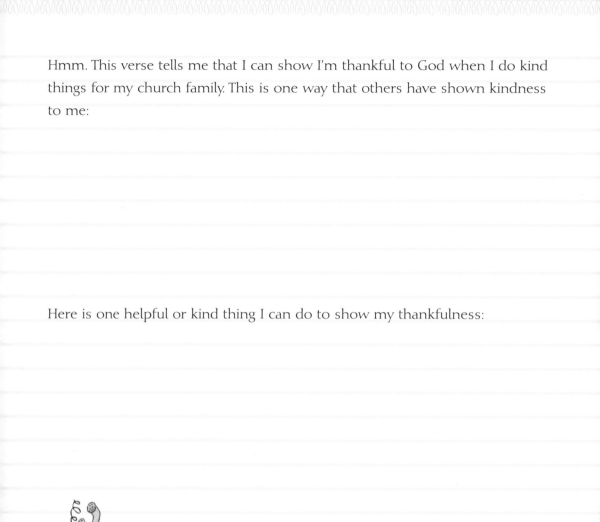

Hmm. This verse tells me that I can show I'm thankful to God when I do kind things for my church family. This is one way that others have shown kindness to me:

Here is one helpful or kind thing I can do to show my thankfulness:

My Prayer

Lord, first of all, I want to thank you for always being there for me. Then I want to say thank you for bringing _____ into my life. Please help me think of some good things I can do to show my thankfulness. Amen.

☀ I like watching Spot swim around in his bowl.

September 16   The Family Secret

Arrrgh. I've got math homework. I don't even see why I have to know stuff like this: $2x + 14 = 30$

This problem had me going through changes until I finally figured out that $x = 8$. Speaking of changes, in 6TH grade there are changes on top of changes. *changes changes* I have more teachers than I've ever had before. In fifth grade I just had Mrs. Lee as my regular teacher, plus Ms. Galbreath for gym and Mr. Sosa for art. Now I have a different teacher for every subject.

Nessa and I are in the same homeroom now. (She wasn't in my room in fourth or fifth grade.) I think God did that because he knew I had been sad about leaving my friends at New Salem Church. Mr. Spivak is our homeroom teacher. He teaches math too. Some of the kids already call him Mr. SPITVAK or SPYvak because you suddenly turn around and there he is looking over your shoulder at your notebook. (I'd rather have him than BOSSY Mrs. Cummings, though. That's who Ronnie has this year.) We meet in our homeroom at the beginning of the day. Then we go to other classes, except for math. That's really different from fifth grade! I feel older and more responsible.

I was trying to make myself look older, but I think I just look stretched out.

Grampa called. Mrs. Huff is getting better. She liked the card I sent her.

There's so much to remember now! We go to different rooms all day. I've got to remember my lunch period (fourth period). And we already have a bunch of homework. Mr. Spyvak (whoops—they've got me calling him that) said that we can always come to him for help with algebra. But he looks kind of mean. He's got these bushy eyebrows and always seems to be frowning. (That's how he seems so far.)

In youth church yesterday I heard some stuff that has really come in handy. The youth pastor—Pastor Jamall—talked about the Holy Spirit. He called the Holy Spirit "the Family Secret." He says that's because we sometimes forget he's there. I know I do. He's like Mr. Spivak (always there) only in a better way. Pastor Jamall says we don't always have to figure stuff out on our own.

I sometimes call the Holy Spirit "the Family Secret" because sometimes we forget he's there.

If the Holy Spirit can help me with sixth grade, maybe he can help me learn to like being at Eagle Rock. Maybe he's been helping me all along. I just didn't realize it. He might be someone I need at church and at school (and at home!). If only he would help me with my math homework!!!

My Thoughts

These are some important things that Leslie needs to remember:

If I were Leslie, I would feel this way about going to my teacher for help:

My Verse

When the Father sends the Counselor as my representative—and by the Counselor I mean the Holy Spirit—he will teach you everything and will remind you of everything I myself have told you.
John 14:26

Hmm. Let me think now of things I need help remembering about God. Some of them are . . .

My Prayer

Jesus, thank you for sending the Holy Spirit to be my helper. Even though I can't see him, I'm glad to know he's always with me! Amen.

September 21 — Leslie to the Rescue

SATURDAY

Even though many things seem to change, some things don't. Lance's
dog, Freedom, tried to escape again. I just happened to look out of
the window in the living room, and I saw Lance run by with a leash
in his hand. When I heard him yelling, "Freedom! Freedom!" I knew
he wasn't on a protest march like Daddy used
to go on back in college.

FREEDOM!

Freedom, come!

Freedom, get over here!

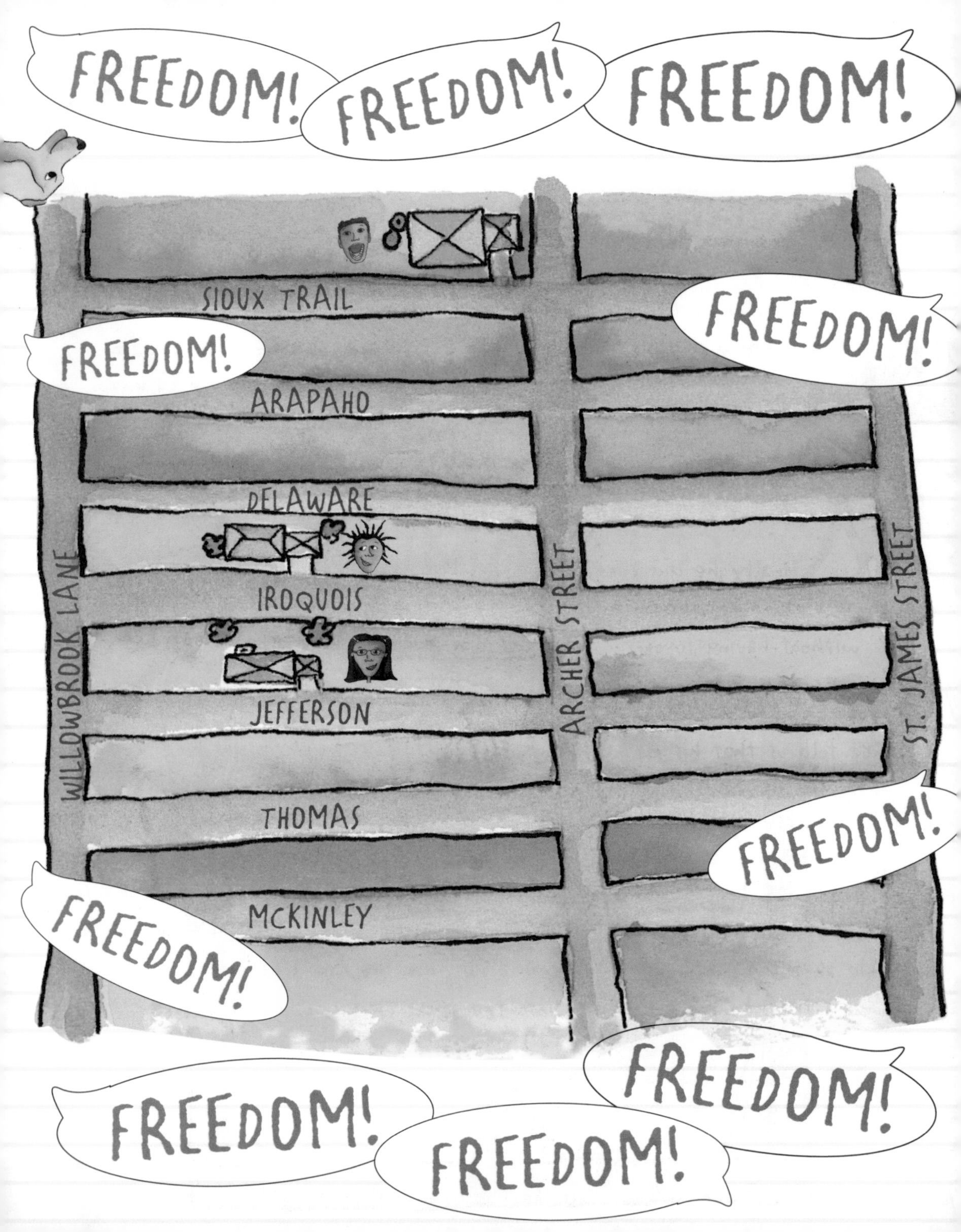
FREEDOM!
FREEDOM!
FREEDOM!
SIOUX TRAIL
FREEDOM!
FREEDOM!
ARAPAHO
DELAWARE
IROQUOIS
JEFFERSON
THOMAS
MCKINLEY
WILLOWBROOK LANE
ARCHER STREET
ST. JAMES STREET
FREEDOM!
FREEDOM!
FREEDOM!
FREEDOM!
FREEDOM!

Freedom is a silly ol' dog. When Lance first got her and she used to escape, I thought she just didn't like being Lance's pet. (I wouldn't blame the dog!) But I've learned that SHE JUST LIKES TO BE CHASED.

I yelled at Ronnie to come take a look outside. Tarita tagged along too, of course. Some of the kids on my block (Halle was there) were already outside laughing at Lance while he chased Freedom in circles around trees. Lance was yelling, "FREEDOM, COME! FREEDOM, GET OVER HERE!" That was so funny! Finally he did the smart thing by asking me for help! Usually, I'm the only one who can catch her. And I do it without having to outrun anybody. (Lance runs faster than me anyway.)

Lance told us that his mother bought a stronger leash for Freedom. But the dog never liked being on a leash.

Ronnie, Lance, and I and some of the other kids on our block chased Freedom down our street (Jefferson). Freedom ran like she had someplace to go. Every now and then she'd stop and look back with her tongue hanging out. Ronnie almost got close enough to grab her, but she faked him out by running around a tree. Ronnie almost ran into the tree. That cracked us all up!

Tarita and her friend Bridget (she calls Bridget "Budgie") kept asking me questions like, "How does Freedom get out? Will Freedom get hurt?" I stopped laughing then. Usually Freedom doesn't get very far. She stays on Lance's block. But here she was three blocks away!! And Archer is a busy street! Lots of cars go down Archer!

Then I felt like maybe I should pray. So I prayed silently. I asked God to keep Freedom from getting hit by a car or getting hurt in any other way.

That's when I came up with the idea to stop chasing Freedom. Instead, I waved her favorite chew toy (a nasty chewed-up rubber thing that had dog slobber on it) in the air. Good thing Lance brought it. As I waved it, I knew I had Freedom's attention. So I nodded to Ronnie to circle around to the left. Freedom came toward me. That's when Ronnie pounced. Lance was there in a second with the leash. Everybody started cheering and saying, "Yeah, girl! Way to go!" and stuff like that. I felt good! Lance told me "Good plan, Cuz-o! I knew I could count on you."

But I knew it was God who had watched out for Freedom. I wish Lance really believed that God cares about stuff. He goes to church, but he's still not a Christian. (I _am_ a Christian. I guess I should ask myself if _I_ always believe that God cares. I know he does, but . . .)

Even though I'm glad some things don't seem to change, maybe some things need to. My aunt and uncle need a new gate, or at least one that closes all the way so that Freedom won't get out.

All summer I've worried about things changing. Now here I am in sixth grade. And we're going to Eagle Rock Bible Church. Sometimes I forget that maybe God cares about all of that too.

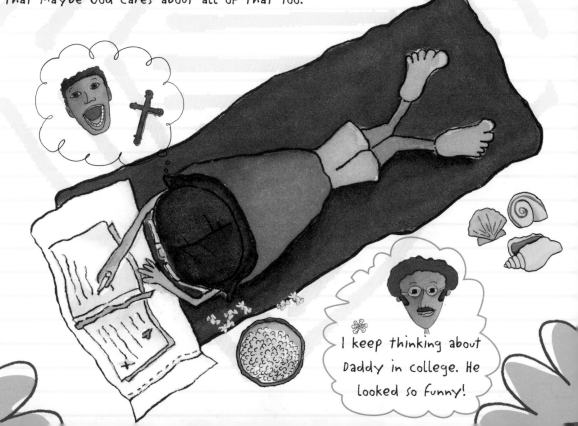

I keep thinking about Daddy in college. He looked so funny!

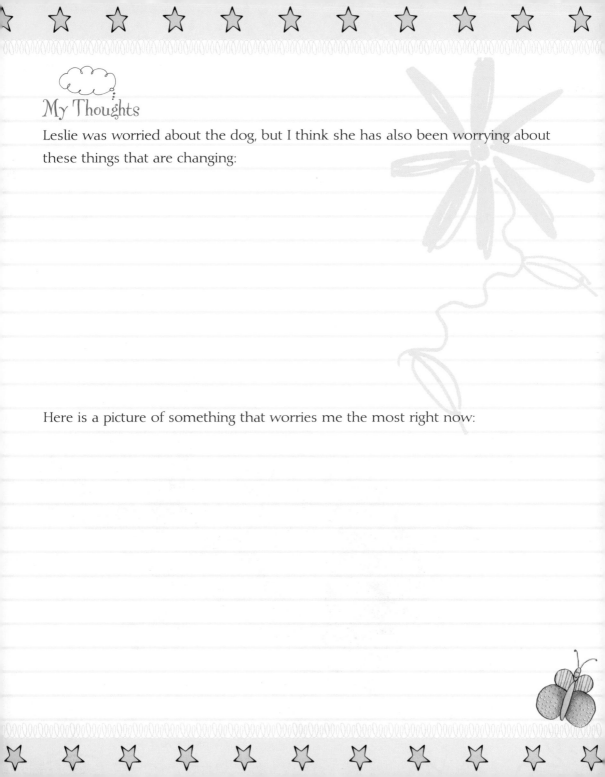

My Thoughts

Leslie was worried about the dog, but I think she has also been worrying about these things that are changing:

Here is a picture of something that worries me the most right now:

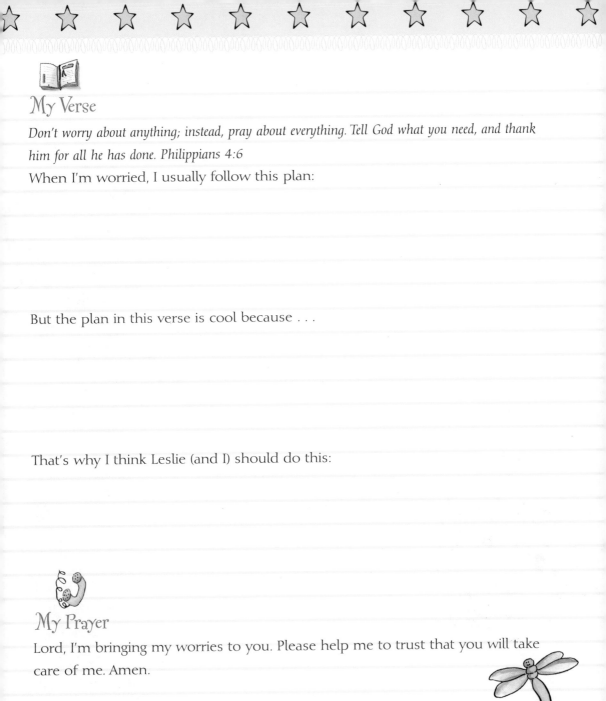

My Verse

Don't worry about anything; instead, pray about everything. Tell God what you need, and thank him for all he has done. Philippians 4:6

When I'm worried, I usually follow this plan:

But the plan in this verse is cool because . . .

That's why I think Leslie (and I) should do this:

My Prayer

Lord, I'm bringing my worries to you. Please help me to trust that you will take care of me. Amen.

September 22   A Part of the Body

Youth church was s-l-a-a-a-a-a-m-m-m-i-n' today! The youth
choir sang a cool song, "CHANGE OF HEART." 💜 It was all
about how God changes people's hearts. Some of the words go

♪ ♩ ♫ ♪ 𝄐

> God can change your way . . . Hey!
>
> God can make your day . . . Say,
>
> God can move your way . . . Today.

That song got everybody clapping. I wish I had written it!
Maybe someday I'll write a song that's just as cool.
I was humming it when I went to find Mama after
youth church. That's when I saw Mrs. Huff in
the hall. When I said hello, she told me

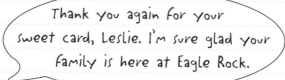

> Thank you again for your
> sweet card, Leslie. I'm sure glad your
> family is here at Eagle Rock.

I'm glad she came back. She looked
better today than she did four weeks
ago. She said nothing could keep her
from God's house.

When I finally found Mama and Daddy, I told them
about the song. Then after we finally found Ronnie
(Tarita was already with us), we went out to eat
at Bun on the Run. (I LOVE THAT PLACE! IT'S
GOT THE BEST BURGERS.) That's when I noticed
Mama and Daddy giving each other "the look". They had been looking at each
other funny ever since I found them after the adult service. I wondered if
something had happened in the service. I nudged Ronnie when I saw them give
each other "the look". All he did was shrug and whisper, "I know I'm not in
trouble. Maybe you are."

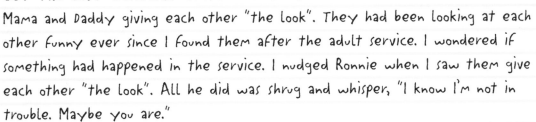

I knew I hadn't done anything. Tarita's been a pest
today (now she's into repeating everything
anybody says),

She's into repeating
everything anybody says!

but she probably hadn't done anything to make
them give each other "the look."

After lunch, I went over to Nessa's for a while. I had
just gotten back home and was about to go watch TV
downstairs when I heard Mama and Daddy in the
basement talking about Eagle Rock.

Well, our four months are almost up. Do you think we made the right decision to leave New Salem so quickly? I'm still not sure Leslie's adjusted to being at Eagle Rock.

Mandi, you know we were uncomfortable about some things at New Salem. Anyway, quit worrying. Let's just ask Leslie how she feels, OK?

I guess they hadn't heard me come into the house. I didn't know whether to go downstairs or go up to my room. Finally I decided I'd go downstairs. But I stopped on my way down, just thinking about what they'd said. I didn't even know they had planned to wait four months before deciding whether we would stay at Eagle Rock. They hadn't said anything to Ronnie, Tarita, or me.

Mama and Daddy were in the family room. Mama asked me how my Sunday school class and youth church were. I just said that both were OK. They looked at each other. Then Daddy asked me if I liked being there. After I thought

It was OK.

about it for a minute, I said yeah. For the first time I really meant it.

I almost laughed at their expressions. They both looked relieved. Daddy waved his open hand at me, then gave me a high five. He told me,

That's my girl!

Mama just hugged me.

When Mama and Daddy first said we were going to Eagle Rock, I was mad. I thought they didn't care how I felt. The song in youth church today helped me realize something. God can change people. God changed my heart about Eagle Rock. I've met some cool people. I never would've met Nicki  and Mrs. Huff if I hadn't come to Eagle Rock. And I like Aubrei and Reesa from Sunday school too. For the first time ever, I think of Eagle Rock as my church.

Mama and Daddy said they want all of us to go through the new members program for families. That's supposed to start this fall. After that maybe I'll think about joining the choir someday even if Regina and her friends are in it. Maybe.

Now if I can adjust to 6ᵀᴴ grade, life will be all the way live!

My Thoughts

In the blank face below I'll draw an expression that shows how Leslie feels now about being at Eagle Rock.

I think it's great that Leslie finally likes being a part of the Eagle Rock church family. I'll use the space below to tell why I think Leslie and her family have decided to stay at Eagle Rock:

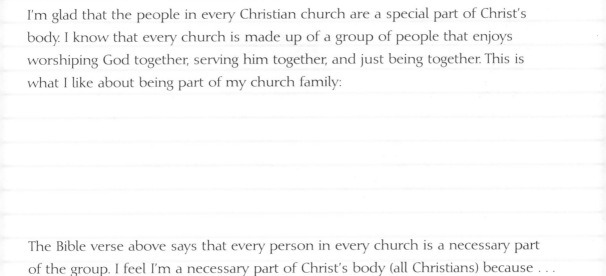

My Verse

Now all of you together are Christ's body, and each one of you is a separate and necessary part of it.
1 Corinthians 12:27

I'm glad that the people in every Christian church are a special part of Christ's body. I know that every church is made up of a group of people that enjoys worshiping God together, serving him together, and just being together. This is what I like about being part of my church family:

The Bible verse above says that every person in every church is a necessary part of the group. I feel I'm a necessary part of Christ's body (all Christians) because . . .

My Prayer

Lord Jesus, I'm glad I'm a part of your body—Christians everywhere. And I'm thankful for my church, where I can worship you and serve you and enjoy being with others who love you. Amen.

About the Author

Linda M. Washington

Linda received a bachelor of arts degree in English from Northwestern University. She has written and edited many books, Bibles, children's devotionals, activity books, and curriculum materials.

Linda has been an editor for Ligature Creative Studios and Cook Communications Ministries. Currently she is a freelance writer and editor for a variety of publishers, and she serves as an editor and writer for "Cool2Read," Tyndale's Web site for kids.

Like Leslie, Linda enjoyed long bike hikes as a kid. And she has chased a dog or two in her day! Linda has always known that she wanted to write, and God has allowed her to do just that. She lives in Carol Stream, Illinois, and enjoys visits with nieces and nephews.

About the Illustrator

Julie (Granite)* Chen

*That was her name before she was married to Sam. He's Chinese.

Julie is an illustrator with a bachelor of fine arts degree from Northern Illinois University. She is also a designer (for a really great Christian publisher), a wife, a daughter, a sister, an aunt, a Bible study leader, and a friend.

Ever since she was a little girl, Julie has wanted to be an artist and a missionary. Now, as the illustrator of her first children's book series, her dreams have come true! To create the art for A Piece of My Mind, Julie used watercolors and India ink, along with a lot of imagination from Linda, the author; Jackie, the designer; and herself.

Julie lives with her husband in northern Illinois.